I Am Their Summer Baby
Copyright © 2022 by Cynthia Jasmine Mora

All rights reserved. No part of this publication
may be reproduced, distributed, or transmitted
in any form or by any means, including
photocopying, recording, or other electronic
or mechanical methods, without the prior
written permission of the author, except in the
case of brief quotations embodied in critical
reviews and certain other non-commercial
uses permitted by copyright law.

Tellwell Talent
www.tellwell.ca

ISBN
978-0-2288-7083-8 (Paperback)

I AM THEIR
SUMMER
BABY

by Cynthia Mora

I am their summer baby.

I have brown hair, brown eyes, and brown skin.

I am funny.

I am smart.

I am happy.

I am a special boy.

July is a special month.

July 20th is my birthday.

Mommy and Mama tell me that I came home on July 24th.

I am so special that I even have balloons and cake for two days in July.

We celebrate for my birthday and we also celebrate for the day I arrived home from the hospital.

Mommy says, "I asked God for a little angel, and He gave me you."

Mama says, "We waited so long for you to come. We tried to keep ourselves busy. We waited and waited and waited."

Then finally I arrived, their summer baby.

I love my family.

Mommy says that all people are special in their own ways. She also says that all families are different. Mama says that even some brothers and sisters do not look alike.

I have a brother and his name is Majesty. We look similar but we are also very different.

I have short hair. He has long hair.

I am short and he is tall.

He has one mom and I have two moms.

Mommy loves to read me books and ask me different questions.

She wants me to be a good listener who pays attention.

She asks, "Where is your head?"

I point to my head.

She asks, "Where is your nose?"

I point to my nose.

She asks, "Where are your stinky feet?"

I point to my stinky feet and chuckle.

Sometimes I zone out and Mommy thinks that I am not listening.

I am listening but I am also distracted by the many beautiful things in my life.

Mama loves to play with me. She sure knows how to have fun.

We play puzzle games, we dance, and we practice boxing. Mama believes that I will be the next boxing champion.

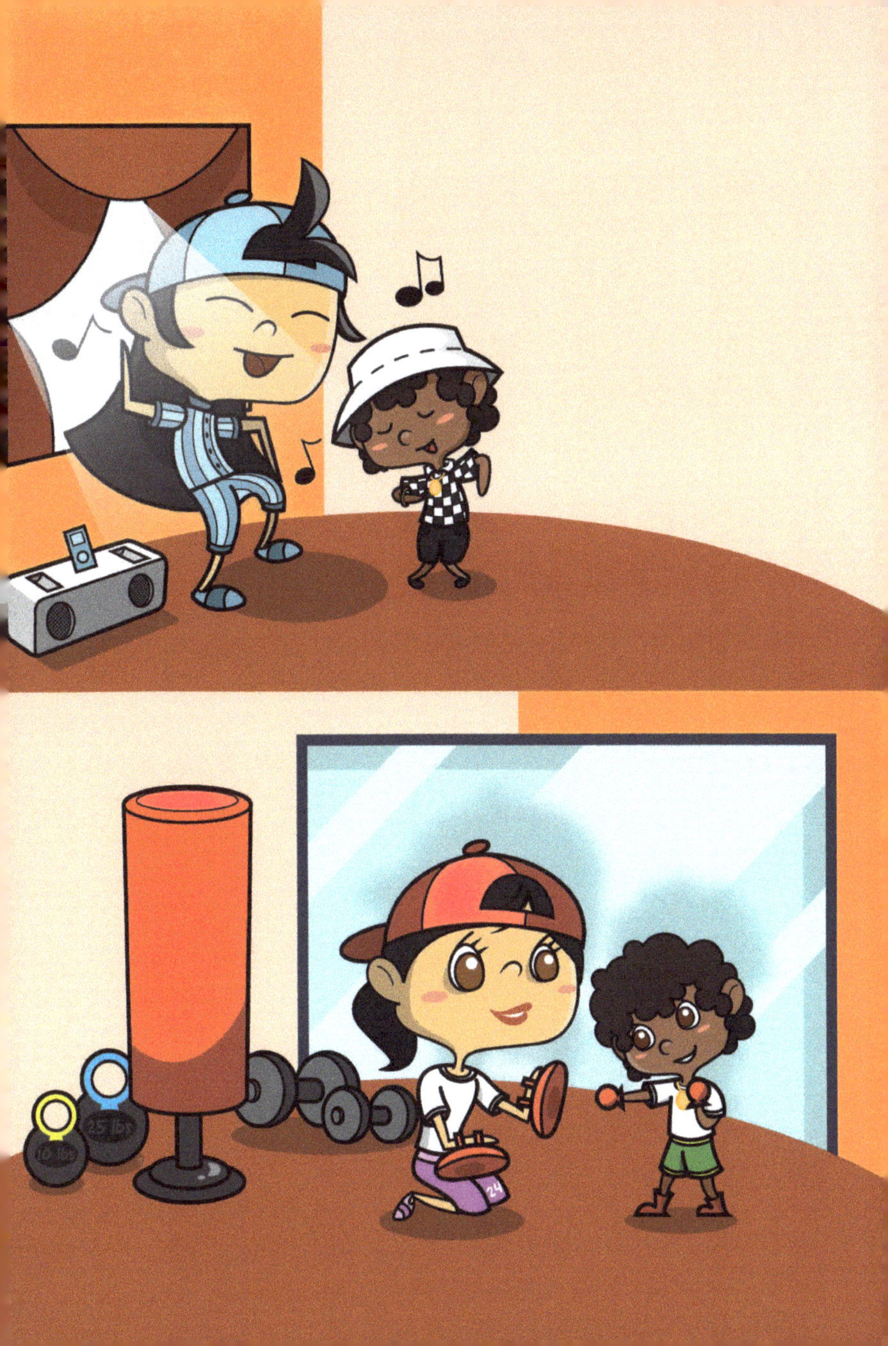

I love my two moms. I am their summer baby.

Some children are born with blue eyes.

Some children are born with brown eyes.

Some children are tall.

Some children are short.

And some children are...

adopted.

I am a special boy.

I have brown hair, brown eyes, and brown skin.

I am funny.

I am smart.

I am happy.

I am adopted.

I am their summer baby.